MW01221983

First published and printed in Canada in 2020
By Shauna-Lee Baty

Editor: Diana Ruff
Front & Back Cover Design: Shauna-Lee Baty
Layout & Design: Amanda Sharp

Weed Your Garden
Paperback ISBN: 978-0-9917778-0-8
e-book ISBN: 978-0-9917778-1-5

Weed Your Garden

By Shauna-Lee Baty

J,

Stay Calm +

Weed On !

Shaun

What to Expect Inside

I want to thank…

My friends. Your support means the world to me. From sharing your stories to thoughtful edits to pep talks, I appreciate your time and heart-felt wishes for a successful journey from my day job!

My son Jordan. You make me want to be a better person. I love you with every cell in my body. Thank you for being you.

My partner Tina. What can I say? Your undying support of my 'craziness' and haphazard ideas, gets me up in the morning. This book could not have been completed without your countless… "Have you written today?" I love you to the moon!

You all make my garden glow with colour and love.

In friendship,

Shauna b

For You

I am dedicating this book to you, the person who is holding this book and reading it's words. You are my inspiration for writing. You understand the true meaning of friendship-otherwise why bother reading this? Am I right? Like myself, you are weeding who is necessary from your garden and planting fresh seeds to blossom. It is the gardening that counts. Tend to your soil, my friend, so you can grow and live a more fulfilling life!

01

Hello –
Good to Meet You

"Let us be grateful to the people who make us happy; they are the charming gardeners who make our souls blossom."

- Marcel Proust

Hello - Good to Meet You

Before we begin, let's all agree on one thing... the people closest to us affect how we think, how we feel, how we make decisions and ultimately our self esteem.

If you don't agree with the above statement, please put his book back on the shelf where someone else will buy it. If you already bought it, first of all-thank you, secondly please pay it forward to someone who is an annoyance in your life. (See what I just did there? Sneaky hey?) Or better yet, gift this to one of your friends that you truly value in your life.

To set things up, in this book I use the analogy of a garden, essentially referring to your social circle of friends and family. The act of 'weeding' your garden means taking care of yourself by purposely getting rid of the toxic people (aka 'weeds') in your life. Your goal is to grow healthy flowers, vegetables, and plants (good people) and eliminate the weeds (toxic people) that stifle their growth. By nature, weeds are persistent, they grow where you don't want them to and they steal the nutrients from surrounding plants. So the question becomes, "How healthy is your garden?" Do you have 'friends' depleting your soil (soul) of nutrients? Are you actually giving these people all your energy and finding in return they rob you of yours? Or perhaps, you weed regularly but they keep popping up when your 'back is turned?' Or maybe, you got rid of a pesky 'weed' but only to find out that weed is now a flower in another's garden! WTF? Deep breath here. For example, you and your best friend have a falling out and she takes root in another of your friend's garden, but this time she is a flower! Hmmm? How does that work? You are familiar with the saying, "One man's junk is another man's treasure." Well, my version of this is "One person's weed is another's flower." For whatever reason or for many reasons that person isn't in line with your 'frequency' or on the same wavelength as you are. But rest assured, it's ok. You are ok. This is a tough one to get your head around, but you are truly better off without them messing up your garden. Trust me, you are better off. And they are too for that matter.

Now time for a little science…

02

Weeds –
A Plant in the Wrong Place.

"A single rose can be my garden... a single friend, my world."

- Leo Buscaglia

Weeds - A Plant in the Wrong Place.

It is estimated that over 8000 plants act as weeds! Notice the phrase - 'act as'? Let's get clear about this. As was illustrated above, some people act as weeds for one person but as a flower (friend) for another. Simply put; she/he was in the wrong place in your garden, but in the right place in someone else's.

I'm going to further illustrate this by bringing science into the discussion. I hope I don't lose any of you here, so hang tight and believe in the process. Or believe in my craziness, whichever feels right for you.

Let's start with the most infamous weed of all time and the bane of any lawn or garden. The Dandelion! Scientifically named *Taraxacum officinale* but more commonly known as the 'Lion's Tooth'. Now, some may argue that the Dandelion is not a pesky weed but indeed a welcomed plant. What?

The Dandelion came to North America from Europe but they are not considered an invasive species by scientists. While you might consider them invasive, they are not by definition. Invasive species of plants aggressively spread and alter natural habitats. Dandelions have a bad rap, but not that bad! There are actually many benefits that dandelions can bring us. To start, they are an important source of food for wildlife. Bees, butterflies and other pollinators rely on the flowers as an early source of pollen and nectar in the Spring. Birds and chipmunks love to eat their leaves. Our local ecosystem is reliant on Dandelions as their pollinators in turn pollinate fruit, vegetables and many other plants important to our own survival. Their broad leaves provide shelter for beneficial insects and even small lizards. With their deep taproots, Dandelions help protect the earth from wind and water erosion. Categorized as a perennial herb, this plant is used for food and healing. Every part, from roots to flower are edible. Ever heard of Dandelion wine? It's a thing. Check it out. Cool, eh? And who can resist picking a seeding dandelion and blowing the seeds everywhere? Not I!

So, you get my point? As with friendships, some people work well in your 'garden' while others spoil the scenery or suck up the nutrients you require for a happy and healthy life. As with the dandelion, is it friend or foe? Only you can decide.

'Weedy Friends'

If you are at a bit of a loss as to who those weeds (negative people) are in your life, then maybe some definitions might help you determine which of your friends you might consider for harvesting. I compiled some familiar and some not-so-familiar terms and catch-phrases that most of us can relate to. I know it's early in this book, but it's time to get real with yourself and your soul (garden). As you read the list below, ask yourself if you have a friend that can be best described by any of these categories, then place their initials beside the number. If you are up for the challenge, then go back through the list and place your initials beside any of the ones that pertain to you. Take a long look in the mirror and be honest with yourself. That's right, shit is gettin' real!

When you are in the company of a person who has the following attributes then, I fully suspect, they need 'weeding' from your garden.

Energy Sucking Leeches

They completely drain you of your energy. Their negative talk is usually about themselves, however, the effect they leave on you is nothing more than depleting all your nutrients and sucking the soil right out of your garden (soul)!

Run Forest Run

You feel attacked, beaten down, drained, and want to leave the minute you meet them.

These people don't have filters, and by this I mean they don't stop to think about what they are saying or doing and *plow* right ahead without regard for your feelings or anyone else's for that matter.

'Debbie Downer' or Eeyore

"Don't blame me if it rains." Their world has a perpetual raincloud hanging over them. For instance, when you refer to the sky as 'Blue' they are convinced it is 'Grey'. Is the grass green to them? Nope - just brown, dying and lifeless. What about the flowers you gave them that you carefully cultivated and harvested and were so proud to give them. "They are just going to die anyway". (And so is this relationship, Eeyore)

The Constant Talker

Without breathing, this person talks non-stop and 'dumps' their shit onto you. (Messy and very unpleasant). They tell you stories about people you don't even know nor do you care to. I have often had 'conversations' with *'Constant Talkers'*, and have literally counted the times that they have asked me even one question. I'm sure you know the answer to this.

The Joker

This is the person who constantly jokes at other people's expense. Hurtful. Not funny at all. This type of person thinks that their mockery of you is fun, witty, and entertaining. Let me tell you, Joker, it ain't funny, so take your BBQ and get the fu@k outta my yard! (reference to an old Monty Python skit). Now that's funny shit, Joker!

The Constant Complainer

Needless to say, we grow weary of these people who seemingly can't or don't want to help themselves. "Oh whoa is me!' The government is to blame. My parents are to blame. The dog is to blame". Wait! Nobody gets to blame the dog! Basically, if these weeds are left unattended, then they become an energy sucking leech. Back to square 1!

Any of these sound familiar? If so, time to get out your spade/shovel (or backhoe in some cases) and start 'weeding' your garden.

Aristotle's Philosophical Point of View

So what does Aristotle have to do with discussing friendship? Isn't he the guy known for theories on politics, ethics, science, etc? Didn't he study under Plato? Wasn't he the guy that taught Alexander the Great? Well, yes he was all those things and much more. Aristotle is lesser known for his philosophy on friendship, but his teachings are more relevant than ever.

He identified three types of friendships: The first two are based on utility and pleasure, and the third one based on mutual appreciation of each other's values. The first two he called 'accidental' friendships, which are limited in depth and don't last very long. But friendships based on virtues and values build the strongest connections and can last for a lifetime.

Utility friendships are those best described by usefulness or convenience. These people could be on the same school board as you or a neighbour we ask to watch the house and water our plants while we slip away for a holiday. These people are what I like to call 'doorstep' friends. You have long chats at their front door but are never invited in. Or you stay a little longer after a meeting to catch up on each other's kids' activities. But once you move away or retire from the board these 'doorstep' friendships quickly dissolve.

Friendships of pleasure are based on enjoyment and having fun together. They give you a 'break' from reality. They could be your 'book' (aka wine) club friend's, Friday night hockey buddies or maybe the people you look forward to seeing at other friends parties. Hugs are always welcome and you bring them as much joy as they offer you. Few demands are expected from each other. These friendships can last a long time.

Lastly, friendships that are based on mutual values, respect and honesty are ever-lasting. This is typically who we might refer to as our BFF's (Best Friend Forever). You may share ups and downs but are steadfast in your conviction to be each other's 'person'. You have shared interests and mutual respect for each other. Likely, your friend's family treats you like one of their own. You may even have a chair of your own at their dinner table. You have both invested a lot of time and effort into each other and will 'fight' for each other should anyone try to cross you. All this from a guy who lived during the 300's BC!

"A friend to all is a friend to none." Aristotle

03

Quiz Time-
Determining the Health of Your 'Garden'.

"Laughter
is not a bad
beginning for
a friendship,
and it is by
far the best
ending
for one."

- Oscar Wilde

Quiz Time

No need to worry, as there are no passes or failures here. This 'quiz' might help you navigate through your garden and determine which plants are weeds and which plants are blossoming. Answer these following questions to help determine whether you need your garden weeded.

When you meet _____ do feel poorly around them?   **Y/N**

When asked to meet with _____ do you make excuses as to why you can't?   **Y/N**

Do you avoid _____ when they try to connect with you?   **Y/N**

Do you find yourself gossiping about _____ to other people?   **Y/N**

After meeting with _____, do you feel like your energy has been drained?   **Y/N**

If you answered 'Yes' to any of the questions above, then maybe you need to take a long, close look at your garden. The people who bring us joy and laughter are the 'flowers' in our gardens. People who bring us down or make us feel uncomfortable are the weeds. Simple right? If it were that simple, then I wouldn't need or want to write this book. *'Stay Calm & Weed On!'* Slb

Are You A Good Friend?

Let's explore a little further into what it means to be a good friend and what a good friend means to you. Thank goodness for the Webster Dictionary for the following:

Friend (Noun) A person whom one knows and with whom one has a bond of mutual affection.

What do friendships mean? Being a friend is beyond just one definition or explanation. It can mean many different things to many different people.

Are you a good friend? Many of us think we are.

What attributes are most important to you in a friend? Take a couple of minutes to jot down your thoughts.

_____

_____

_____

_____

_____

_____

_____

Any of your answers surprise you? It can be a difficult question because most of us go throughout life without giving much thought to it. The point I really want to make here is we all have similar values and expectations of our friends. We hold these attributes high over their heads. So I ask you now, *"Do you hold yourself accountable to these same attributes?"*

Take stock of the following top five attributes from the people I interviewed when asked, 'what they thought made a good friend.'

Female answers:

Attribute 1. Honesty, #1 by a mile!

Attribute 2. Punctual-respectful of one's time.

Attribute 3. Treated as an equal.

Attribute 4. Listens with respect.

Attribute 5. Zest for learning and evolving as a person.

Male answers:

Attribute 1. Honesty, #1 again.

Attribute 2. Fun to be around.

Attribute 3. Share things in common.

Attribute 4. Kind.

Attribute 5. Funny.

I'm going to make the assumption that many of the above attributes match your list as well. Many of us are similar in our idealism of what kind of friends we like to have in our garden. But back to you. Tough question ahead so hang on tight…

Again, "Are you a good friend?" Of that list you produced, what attributes describe you? What attributes do you honestly feel your friends would write down about you? It's been said time and again, "You can't have good friends until you are one."

Get real with yourself. If you really want to better yourself and your relationships, ask your close friends what they think are your attributes and be prepared for the truth. If your thoughts are different from theirs, then its time to reevaluate what is going on. Grab this book and one for them as well and make a 'date' to sit down with them. This takes strength, determination and courage, but isn't it worth it?

04

A Reason,
A Season,
A Lifetime

"There is magic in long-distance friendships. They let you relate to other human beings in a way that goes beyond being physically together and is often more profound."

- Diana Cortes

A Reason, A Season, A Lifetime

There is a poem that I have referred to many times over the years to help explain what different friends have meant to me. Enjoy.

People come into your life for a reason,
a season or a lifetime.

When you figure out which one it is, you will know what to do for each person.

*When someone is in your life for a **reason** it is usually to meet a need you have expressed. They have come to assist you through a difficulty; to provide you with guidance and support; to aid you physically, emotionally or spiritually. They may seem like a godsend, and they are. They are only there for the reason you need them to be.*

Then, without any wrongdoing on your part or at an inconvenient time, this person will say or do something to bring the relationship to an end. Sometimes they die. Sometimes they walk away. Sometimes they act up and force you to take a stand. What we must realize is that our need has been met, our desire fulfilled; their work is done. The prayer you have set up is answered and now it is time to move on.

*Some people come into your life for a **season**, because your turn has come to share, grow or learn. They bring you an experience of peace or make you laugh.*

They may teach you something you have never done. They usually give you an unbelievable amount of joy. Believe it. It is real. But only for a season.

***Lifetime** relationships teach you lifetime lessons; things you must build upon in order to have a solid emotional foundation. Your job is to accept the lesson, love the person, and put what you have learned to use in all other relationships and areas of your life.*

It is said that love is blind but friendship is clairvoyant.

- unknown

Wow! What a great passage explaining the fundamentals of friendship. In keeping with the theme of this book, I decided to link the above categories with the following:

A bouquet of flowers = *a Reason*.

Annuals = *a Season*.

Perennials = *a Lifetime*.

Lets dig a little deeper into meanings

A bouquet of flowers typically lasts about a week. For most of us, when we receive flowers, they put a smile on our faces because we realize that someone is paying attention to us. We love the colors, the aromas, the added foliage to make it look pretty. Maybe they came in a pretty paper wrap or a vase that you get to use again. But we still have to face it, that these will not last long. They are meant to serve a purpose. They may survive a couple days longer if we attend to them daily with fresh water and pruning. But, we are only extending their beauty for a short time. Eventually, they end up in the compost.

The reasons for giving or receiving a bouquet are too many to list, but I'll give it a go anyhow.

~ You broke your ankle while trying out the mechanical bull at the local rodeo. Next time, maybe just watch your friends take the hit- send them flowers instead.

~ You graduated from high school and Aunt Ella sent you roses because her place smells like them all the time.

~ You forgot your wife's birthday, her work anniversary, the completion of her first Spanish course (Olé), her running in her 15th triathlon, your anniversary (better be an expensive bouquet)! This list is endless, sorry guys (and gals in some situations).

~ Your boss recognized a 'job well done'.

~ You moved into a new home.

~ Someone close to you passed away and someone wanted to recognize your loss.

~ You fed your neighbour's cat for two weeks while they traveled to Europe and they brought you back a Gnome from Switzerland and, you guessed it, flowers.

You get the picture.

But, on the flip side, some people think sending or receiving flowers is a waste of time. Their reasoning is that the flowers only last for a short time then they have to get rid of them because they die. No smiles. No excitement. No mystery. No smells.

So what if we took those same thoughts and translated them to people? What might that look like? The 'Reason' people would be void from your life. So what? I mean, what's the point of having someone in your life for such a short period of time? Right?

Not so fast Batman! The reason that the 'Reason' people come into your life is just that. A reason. One reason. Not two or three or more, because that is what the 'Season' people are for-one reason only. I liken these people to 'gypsies'. They flow in, they flow out. They are on the move. Not to get confused with people actually moving away from where you live, but people who are in your life for a brief moment.

For example, perhaps you had a divorce. Maybe that 'Reason' friend helped you through this tough time. They texted you every morning with a happy emoji face or they picked you up to take you out when you didn't want to leave the warm sheets of your bed. They made you get dressed and go for a brisk walk or a coffee in a public place away from the memories that surrounded you 24/7. They could have referred a lawyer to you or helped baby sit the kids while you got stuff done. And then, like a flash, they are gone. Their role is complete. Or maybe you and your ex decided to make things work. Poof-gone. People tend not to want to stick around if they feel their 'work' is not appreciated. In this example, your 'reason friend' basically feels "f@ck you and all the crying I put up with and your screaming kids, and you can have your douche bag husband back. You deserve each other!" Or something like that. The flowers need to be thrown out, nonetheless.

Another common example of a 'reason' friend is that one person who shows up when you least expect it, but you have very deep and meaningful conversations and together you solve all the world problems in a single night! You feel energized, jazzed up (just like energized but a cooler word)! You laugh a lot, you feel you can run the company on your own or you are going to go out and get that client that you've had your eye on for months. Whatever it is, you feel like a Super-person (politically correct). "We will get together for dinner soon, I'll have a bbq and you're on the top of the list." But lets face it, this never happens, it won't happen so get over it. "The road is paved with good intentions." We both know that this road will remain a dirt road less travelled. BUT. BUTT! The feelings remain solid. The thoughts about your connection remains strong. You have good thoughts about your 'Reason' friend because you know you will bump into them again and have another great time. The 'flowers' can be tossed but keep the vase for next time!

Many years ago, my partner at the time cheated on me. She had an affair and I was devastated. So my friends rallied around me to ensure I wouldn't fall into an abyss and never be seen again. I remember meeting T.B. soon after this. She was young and fun and was very supportive. I would spend a lot of time crying on her shoulder and talking through the whole ordeal. She helped me out immensely. But the one thing that stands out for me was her ability to energize me. Or I should say, I was ener-gized by her energy. I slowly regained my own energy source and confidence back. A few months later I was dating again and feeling great. But where did T.B. go? I tried on several occasions to bring her back into the fold, but she kept distancing herself from me. I never got an answer from her as to why she disappeared. So, I made my own conclusion - I chalked it up to jealousy. That's right, jealousy. I actually hate that word because the mere definition of the word is laced with fear, anger, and resentment.

These feelings don't bode well with me. At the time I thought 'She should be happy for me, I mean I'm getting on with my life, I'm happy and I'm exploring new relationships.' Right? Wrong. I'll never really know why she left but I do thank her from the bottom of my heart. Hey, T.B. if you are out there or you are reading this - big hugs!!

Annual. Adjective: Occurring once every year.

By its true nature, an annual lasts only a year and it perpetuates itself by seed. Any gardener knows that every year they are heading to the nursery to buy their annuals for the season. They load up the cart in the spring and then enjoy the plants and flowers for a few months only to then turn around and dig them up as fall and winter approach. If you live in Canada, like I do, then you know this season is grossly shortened!

Ok, so how does this relate to friendship? A 'Season' friend is someone who helps us grow and learn, almost at an exponential rate. But again, they don't last for a long time in our lives. Much like the annual flowers you purchase, they bring you great joy but for a limited time. These people are in our lives because we need a boost or rocket fuel to help us grow. Perhaps this person(s) is working in an industry that you have always been interested in but didn't have the confidence in pursuing. She brings you experiences of her own that help you formulate a plan to get you there as well. She is well

42

networked and shares her connections with you, thereby saving you time and money sourcing out on your own. She can even get you an interview with her boss or a co-worker who has influence in the company. Often, this 'Season' friend will socialize with you and introduce you to a new way of thinking. You are excited. You have a new zest for life. You wake up thinking of your 'luck' in meeting her. What a blessing! You are now on your way to realizing that your dreams can come true. Will come true. Then one day you wake up and your flowers are wilted or have a bug devouring its leaves that you can't stop. Now what? Where did she go? Her job is done. The season is over. You may feel hurt or left wondering why did she leave? Or maybe, you left first. You got what you needed and now you are self-sufficient. On your own. Able to leap tall buildings in a single bound! Never forgotten. Always in your heart. Just not in your life.

The snow has fallen (or monsoon season has started - completely dependent upon which hemisphere you live in). You get my point.

Perennial. Adjective: *Lasting or existing for a long or apparently infinite time; enduring or continually recurring. Permanently engaged in a specified role or way of life.*

So, like perennial plants, some friends stick around for a long time. Make no mistake, these people are invested in you. And you should be invested in them as well. Why? These people are intertwined in your life and you in theirs, so much so that their absence would gravely affect your life. And visa versa of course. As the poem suggests, you have built a solid foundation over the years with these people. Much time, effort, and emotional involvement has been extended over many years. Your lives are so interwoven it would seem weird not to have them in your life. These people are vibrating on the same frequency as yours. You just get each other. Sometimes you can go weeks, or even months without contact, but then pick up where you left off as if no time has passed.

One friend of mine, in particular, comes to mind as an example. S.L. and I met in our mid twenties. Just starting our careers in the pharmaceutical industry, we trained together and have been friends since. She lives in a different city than I, but our friendship hasn't wavered. We can go weeks without contact but never lose touch. Why is this? Don't we need more time or communication to keep our friendship intact? As a matter of fact, I find my relationship with her 'easy'.

A 'perennial' plant requires most of its energy growing and thriving in the first few years of planting. Once it reaches maturity, it generally needs little attention beyond some pruning and occasional fertilizing. So liken this to a lasting friendship. Much of the attention is required at the beginning. You are getting to know each other, spending time together and sharing all your life's ambitions. Much like the 'Season' friend, when you meet your 'Lifetime' friend you are excited, energized and enjoy your time with them. At the onset, you can't tell the difference between these types of friends. What sets them apart is longevity and persistent value. The 'Lifetime' friend can be one for a lifetime but also can be one for a very long time but something eventually separates you both. Should this friend be there until death do you part?

Not necessarily. Let's figure this out.

First of all, no one can predict how long any relationship will last. Even marriages that have a contract drawn up, can fail. All you have to do is look at the stats. Anywhere from 40% to over 60% of marriages end up in separation or divorce. So how can we think that our friendships will last as long if not forever? No contracts were written or signed. No ceremony declaring your undying love and devotion was performed. No flower petals or rice thrown at you both happened. Wait. There may be a limo involved, but likely when you are on a bar hopping tour. Fun hey?

Many of us expect that 'Lifetime' friends will last as long as we like. But most don't. Again, these friendships teach us lifetime lessons but may not last a lifetime. Does this make sense? Kinda? Sorta? Not really? As you grow throughout your lifetime, some people will grow with you. As long as your values remain the same and you have a number of things in common, then the relationship will last. If you find that your values change from theirs or that you have less and less in common, then likely you will part ways. Or at the very least, you will remain 'friendly' with each other but unlikely stay in touch much. Slowly drifting apart but always thankful for the life lessons learned and retained.

As in the case of my 'Lifetime' friend, S.L. we have a lot in common and share persistent values. We have both moved on from the Pharma world into the entrepreneurial world. We have always supported each other in our personal endeavours. Although our occupations have nothing in common, we share our need to succeed on the goals we set forth. We, most recently, are exploring the world of digital engagement together. After having a life time of experiences, we are working on capturing our talents and sharing with the world online. Stay tuned.

As for the values we share, they are persistent. They really haven't moved off the needle much. She and I value honesty, integrity and wholesomeness, amongst many other attributes. I love her deeply. I respect her beyond words. I am honoured to call her my friend. Thirty years and still going strong!!

05

From the Beginning - Beginning - My Personal Journey

"One of the most toxic things I've done is ignore the bad in someone because I wanted to keep them in my life."

- 3am Thoughts

From the Beginning, My Personal Journey

Before I even began writing this book, I jotted down several titles that I thought would best describe what I was trying to convey. (Imagine a sketchpad with scribbles of words not formulated into sentences)

Weeding your garden - How to get rid of people in your life.

How to get rid of annoying people in your life.

DNA is not a good enough reason… to keep them in your life

   ~ Choosing friends and family for your life.

Don't text me back!

   ~ and other meaningful ways to tell people to f@ck off!

Piss off! - for good.

   ~ A reasonable guide for getting rid of people you no longer want in your life.

"Off My List"

Getting rid of poisonous people - without killing them.

Control X

Delete

...I could go on.

The above working titles were a compilation of ideas, thoughts, and experiences I have had throughout my life here on Earth. Instead of bitching to my partner or reposting pictures on Instagram about how difficult it is to put up with difficult people, I have decided to write everything out in plain English (or a reasonable variation of this language).

A few years ago a friend of mine (who now resides in my 'Weeded' category, for several reasons) explained to me that she had had to, "from time to time, get rid of people in her life because they were poison, because their energy was negative and brought her down."

Well, I am taking this sage advice and now capturing it here in this writing.

The other catalyst for writing this book was my separation after 20 years. (seems like another book required)? I always thought that no matter what shit might come down between my ex and I, our friends would rally around us and support both of us. Boy was I wrong! Not only was there no rally, there weren't even any phone calls from any or our 'friends' reaching out to see how they could help. What I actually got was nothing. That's right. A big, fat dose of NOTHING! They all disappeared from my life. It was an even more impressive disappearing act than Houdini pulled off. Not a word. Not a whisper. Not even a sideways glance. I was 'weeded' from their gardens for good. BUT, and I mean a BIG ASS BUTT inserted here, BUT they all did me an amazing favour. I mean, it freed up storage space on my cell phone as I delightfully deleted every one of them from my contact list, Instagram, Facebook, and my life! Have you ever felt really good when you cleaned out your closet or garage? Have you ever followed the Marie Kondo steps to creating a life of more Joy and less clutter? How about unmessing your thoughts as Gary Bishop points out in his book, 'Unfu*k Yourself?' Well, for me, this was like taking all of that combined with the Titanic (we all know how that ended) and all the dinosaurs that ever roamed this Earth (didn't end well for them either) and then tossing them all out the window, for good! Yes, once I reframed what had happened, I never felt more free!! I cleansed these people from my phone, but more importantly, my soul. And that folks, is what I call 'weeding my garden.' I got rid of a large collection of toxicity and now only flowers grow in my garden, with the occasional weed that blows in from time to time.

They say, 'You can choose your friends but not your family.' Well, that's not entirely accurate, is it? Let me explain.

At the age of two years, my 'father' (commonly referred by me as my sperm donor) kicked my sister, mom and I out of the house we were supposed to grow up in. That's right. As we were leaving out the front door, his new girlfriend and her daughter were moving in through the back door! The first moment my mom was aware that anything going on was when she heard a knock on the door and upon opening it, she was served divorce papers! I can't even imagine how she felt in that moment. I suspect she felt like she was hit by a Mac truck. Drained of all energy. Confused, hurt, betrayed, lost. She was faced with enormous challenges for years after that single moment.

She packed up what little she could and we moved into a friend's house. We lived there for four and a half years until mom was in a position to rent a place for the three of us to live in. She had a hard time securing a job, as back in those days you had to put your marital status on your resume. And the word 'Divorced' was simply not acceptable. I mean as a divorced woman somehow it was your fault your husband was an asshole and left you and your kids stranded!

I didn't realize how this had impacted me until quite recently. I'm 54 years old now and just starting to understand the impact. The word that keeps resonating with me is *'abandonment'*. I've used this word quite loosely over the years without much regard. BUT NOW? Its all starting to make sense.

On a recent trip to Mexico, I met a lovely couple over drinks and we struck up a conversation about writing. Steve was in the process of using a ghost writer to help him share his story of how he only hired ex-cons in his business and how they greatly impacted his life. His working book title is 'Second Chances.' Appropriately named.

He then asked me if I was writing this book for the millions $$$ I will receive - LOL. Without a blink I answered, *"No. I'm writing to find answers."*

It is with my sincerest hope that these following pages help you and I find the answers to create a better life with people that truly help us to become our better selves.

Now, on with the fun stuff!

06

Storytime...

"You teach people how to treat you."

- Anon

Storytime

Throughout this book you will find several stories that most of us can relate to. While some may be sad in nature or thought-provoking or even humorous, they are all true accounts of people willing to share their experiences with me, and now you, in order to create a better understanding of their own world. Here are my top three stories that have helped shape my life, to this point.

STORY#1. Lessons From My 9 year old.

My son, at the time, was in grade 5 when he started to have girl 'crushes'. Nothing serious, but not to be taken too lightly either. His first 'girlfriend' would text him constantly through-out the day and early mornings of school. "Can you meet me at the back stairs by the bike rack?" "Sure," was his reply. (Not kidding about the bike rack).

She would go on and on about 'nothing' to which he had one of three responses:

~ "Sure"

~ "Ok"

~ "Yup"

He soon grew tired of this 'annoyance' and decided to text her the following:

"Stop texting me, I don't like you anymore"

WTF? (my response)

I was immediately on him about his abrupt text and seemingly rude methodology.

"You can't text her that!" I was on him.

"Why not?" He asked.

I started to explain how girls can be quite emotional and how this could really upset her and hurt her, etc. I went on and on… (much like the texts he was getting).

After he took in all that I had to give him, he turned to me and said - "Na, I still don't like her anymore, so I'm just being honest," to which he walked away leaving me speechless.

I was schooled.

I must point out here that both my son and I are what John Grey would call, 'Martians'*. I reference his book here as it explains very well how different people respond to different situations. A must read if you haven't by now.

Fast forward to today. My son is now in Sr high School and has had a few girlfriends and he continues to break up in the same manner… "Mom I don't like her anymore."

Have I raised a monster? Quite the contrary. He is becoming the person I admire - confident, self assured, caring, thoughtful, etc. He just deals with matters from a very practical approach. A 'Martian'.

This story was the catalyst to my writing this book. He was my teacher and in many ways continues to be. I have so many times wanted to just text people to tell them they are off 'My List'. But it seems harder than that. Right? (Venus is present).

"It really isn't Mom."

* *Men Are From Mars, Women Are From Venus* - John Grey

STORY #2. One of My First Experiences...
Breaking up with boys

I'm going to take you back, way back, to Jr High School. I had several 'boy friends' while in school. Having several boyfriends meant several break ups. Now you have to understand this took place at a time in history when the World Wide Web hadn't been invented yet. Cell phones didn't even enter into our vocabulary. Color TV had just started making it into homes (you were considered privileged to even own a TV). So basically we communicated by either phone (the kind attached to the wall) or writing.

It is important to note that one's ability to deal with break-ups is solely based on one's maturity level-how you deal with things as a teenager vs adult is quite different. I mean teenagers are emotional, ego-based, disrespect-ful, shy, all-knowing, secretive, etc. Adults are just the opposite. Right? WRONG!!!!! Basically all the above applies to adults as well. That's right. You know it deep down. Just think of the last time you got 'dumped' or you did the dumping. Countless friends of mine over the years have gone off the deep end. We turn into 'bitches from hell' or complete jerks when we go through these experiences.

Let's return to the main focus of this writing. What did I do when I was 13 and didn't want said boyfriend around any more? What any teenage girl would respectfully do - ask my best friend to tell 'boyfriend' that I was no lon-ger 'going around' with him. (back then this was a thing-trust me, just go with it).

Today things are not that different. Teenagers communicate through text, Snapchat, i-mes-sage, DM on Instagram, Facebook, etc. The message gets across just the same, *I am no longer interested in having you in my life. Please delete me from all your social media.* Or some variation on the theme with a lot fewer words.

The mode of the break up may be quite dif-ferent now from then, but the intention is the same… "Weeding My Garden".

STORY #3. To weed or not to weed… what is the question?

This story began when I was in my mid-twen-ties and continued for about 25 years. When I graduated from University I set my sights on working in the Pharmaceutical industry. Back then this meant a lot of travel, way too much drinking and the occasional 'hard work' day.

I met a colleague from Ottawa, Ontario who was my roommate at one of my very first meetings in Toronto. We hit it off. She was fun, lively, smart and a genuinely good person. I still believe she is the same person today as she was back then. We travelled together, talked regularly, shared each other's ups and downs. She left the company a couple of years later, but we stayed friends. One day I got a call from her asking me if I wanted to join her on a company trip she won as a rep. It was a trip to the Bahamas, so of course I said yes and was soon on a plane.

The first night we were there was a huge company dinner. All the 'brass', managers, representatives etc were there. It is important to note that these trips included free alcohol and parties every night. So CS, who was not a big drinker, somehow got herself into trouble quickly when I found her 'kissing the porcelain'. (throwing up in the toilet). So I got her out of the restaurant to avoid further embarrassment. That night I stayed up holding her hair back each time she dry heaved into the waste basket. What are friends for, right?

Needless to say, she was in no shape to take a snorkelling boat over to the coral reefs the next day. So I left her with some food and Advil, and joined the rest of the crew for the day. When I returned to our room I was met with a very cold shoulder. She finally told me she was pissed off that I went on the tour. What was I supposed to do? Stay behind while she slept all day? No thanks.

So the remaining of the week there was difficult but I made the most of it. I met some fun people and hung with them. She and I were 'ok' with each other but something changed. Till this day, I still don't know what set her off. We didn't talk for months afterwards (I felt my roots being torn right out of the ground). Was I weeded?

Interestingly enough I ended up working for this same company (Pfizer) a couple of years later. So we reunited, C.S. and I, and we picked up where we left off-both choosing to not talk about the incident as if it never happened.

We kept in touch for many years. The calls were regular but less meaningful - for me. She would always call me when she had 'get rich quick' ideas and wanted me to jump on the band wagon. Or when she had another bad break up with another boyfriend. Or when she found out her soon to be husband was married and living in the States. (This after she gave him all her saved up money to help him with his 'business'). She cried on my shoulder(s) for many years.

I was not enjoying her as a friend any longer, so I stopped the calls and texts to her. Only a couple of years ago, she reached out to me again. I stared at my cell phone as it rang. I didn't want to answer it. She left me another message of a "great company to invest in, you should call me".

I didn't.

That relationship was put to bed. Plucked from my garden, where only flowers grow now.

07

Digging Deep Into Your Garden,

The Root of the Matter

If you live to be 100, I hope I live to be 100 minus 1 day, so I never have to live without you.

- Winnie the Pooh

Digging Deep Into Your Garden, The Root of the Matter

In this chapter, let's explore how sometimes, long lasting and deep rooted friendships can be harmful to our own personal growth. Take the 'Thistle' weed for example. It has long deep roots embedded in the ground and is known for how stubborn it is to get rid of (anyone come to mind)?

A little more science…

Non-native thistles arrived as weed seeds in North America quite by accident. They were 'stow-aways' on ships in either crop seeds or in the ballasts of ships. They have become major problems in agricultural landscapes and many agriculturalists have designated them as noxious weeds. Some thistles even release chemicals into the soil that inhibit the growth of other plants. They tend to take hold in disturbed soils. As an opportunist plant, it can grow almost anywhere and in any soil condition. Beyond your back yard, these opportunists can take hold in fields and road ditches, wet and dry places, and mountain pastures. However, on the up-side, thistles do attract pollinators and birds. Once again, friend or foe?

Here are some fun facts about Thistles:

- The Thistle is a national symbol of Scotland and is well known for its sharp, prickly nature. It is oldest recorded 'National Flower' dating back to the 13th century. Legend has it that when the Vikings tried to sneak up on Scottish Clansmen, they walked barefoot over thistles. Their cries of pain alerted the Scottish army and not surprising, it didn't end well for these folks.

- The thistle flower grows its spiny leaves to protect against being eaten by wildlife. Mother Nature is so clever.

- Edible thistles, such as the bull thistle, can be roasted and enjoyed in a salad, for instance, while its seeds can be used for producing oil.

- Thistles bloom in a range of colours including yellow and white, however, they are most commonly seen in shades of purple.

Ok, back to humans. Have you ever struggled within a friendship that you have been involved in for many years and you know it's not good for your soul, yet it continues to stick around, like a thistle? Ever feel trapped, like you really don't find pleasure in this person, but don't know how to end it? (insert deep breath here). I've heard countless times from people, particularly women, who complain that their life-long friendship(s) are turning into life-long headaches. *Can I have a high-5 here? Don't leave me hanging! It's embarrassing, not to mention tiring.*

"There is nothing better than a friend, unless it's a friend with" chocolate.

- Linda Grayson

Storytime...

Perhaps a few stories might shed some light on these types of relationships. As you read along, keep in touch with how you are 'feeling' as opposed to what you 'think' about these situations. If you can relate to these people at all, write down your feelings that you are experiencing. Write down what part of your body is affected. What is it telling you? For example, do you feel a pit in your stomach when you think of person X? Do you get anxious or nervous when you are making plans to meet with her/him? Do you feel sad knowing that your friendship isn't the same as it was years ago? Would you feel a sense of failure if your friendship came to an end? Use these questions as a barometer to 'test' how you are currently perceiving your friendship(s). And remember, jot down anything that comes to mind, even if it doesn't make sense right now. You can always analyze later.

_____

_____

_____

_____

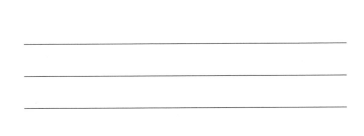

'Friendship isn't about who you've known the longest. It's about who walked into your life, said, "I'm here for you" and proved it.' Anon.

STORY # 4. "I feel sorry for her."

My friend CS shared her thoughts and feelings with me about a friendship she has been struggling with for several years. Her friend in question would best be classified as a *'Constant Complainer'*.

'JJ' is described by CS as someone who never stops talking about herself, regularly changes plans without notice and who 'milks the system' for everything it's got. "Why do I keep this relationship?" CS asked me - not expecting an answer but hopeful for one. "We really aren't on the same frequency or wavelength, "she went on to explain. "I'm a go-getter and I am very active in my business. I've always set goals and work hard to achieve them. Someone like JJ expects things to be handed out to her. She does the bare minimum to get by and expects government handouts to pay her bills". "It's really a one-way relationship,"

CS explained. "I actually don't reach out to her anymore. She contacts me and then I go along with the plan." I asked her why she doesn't just confront JJ. CS said she really doesn't know the answer, but did say she felt sorry for her. "She lost a son and I feel bad for her, so I don't want to hurt her feelings". So this story will end with a... to be continued.

Let's break it down.

Do you have any friendships that resemble the friendship between CS and JJ? What did you do to change things or end it or are you still on the treadmill and can't get off it? Regardless of your situation, take stock of what value you are getting from your friendship. This is a good place to write down some of your answers to these questions.

_____

_____

_____

_____

Are you 'growing' apart from a friend?

Raise your hand if you are wondering if something is up with your friend. If you are getting those butterflies in your tummy (as opposed to your garden) then take note of what's going on around you. For instance, if your friend constantly cancels plans or 'ghosts' you on texting then don't ignore these actions. Something is going on, even if you can't put your (green thumb) finger on it!

STORY #5. Since Grade 9

TT shared a story about a friend of hers that has left her questioning the value of their relationship. Let's explore some details so we can get more clarity on the subject of longevity between friends.

TT and SJ met in Junior High school in grade 9. They became fast friends and have maintained this relationship for close to 30 years. As typical teenage friends, they were inseparable. They hung out everyday and when they weren't together, they were on the phone with each other constantly. In mid high school, TT moved to another city but they still kept up the close contact. Texting each other was an every day occurrence. They would also travel to see each other 3-4 times per year and pick up where they left off.

The story gets a little fuzzy as TT recounts situations leading up to the present time-or at least up to the time of publishing. For example, TT and SJ have made plans to meet on several occasions during the last three years and have had the plans fall through. TT says its not due to anything on her end. One instance, she recalls that SJ was coming to her home town so they made plans to meet at a local restaurant. As the evening wore on, SJ did not call or text TT to let her know she would not be able to make it. Needless to say, TT was extremely hurt and disappointed that her life-long friend couldn't even bother to text her that the plans fell through. Her excuse the next day was, "I was so drunk, I forgot to text you." Lame? Yes.

It was quite some time before they resumed communication. But it was solely through texting or Snapchat videos to each other complete with cat ears and whiskers. If you don't get what Snapchat video or pictures are, well you're not alone. But each to his/her own. Who am I to judge?

The most recent problem happened when they were both going on separate vacations to Mexico and realized they would be there at the same time. So the plan was to meet up as it was a simple cab ride away. Can you guess what happened? I'll give you a minute to ponder…

Well, I'm sure you guessed it. TT got to Mexico and reached out to SJ to make plans, only to find out SJ had already gone back home to Canada. No text, no phone call, no email, no nothing from SJ!

"I'm sick of her treating me this way. I mean, I go out of my way to accommodate plans with her, and yet she can't even be bothered to let me know," TT explained. So I asked her how she now describes SJ. "Disrespectful, rude and inconsiderate, she answered quickly.

"So now what are you going to do about it?" I asked.

"I'm going to give her one last chance. We've made plans to meet in a couple of months and if she bails on me then I'm calling it quits. No more texting or Snap-chatting or communication of any kind. Friends don't treat friends this way." TT answered confidently.

So again, as with the last story, we will have to settle for a… To be continued.

Break it down some more.

Do you have a friend that is seemingly stringing you along? They give you just enough attention to hold your attention, but the substance of a good relationship is gone. Is it enough for you? Or are you constantly 'fighting' to keep whatever is left? Why do you think you are hanging on? Jot down your ideas/thoughts/feelings about this.

_____

_____

_____

_____

_____

_____

_____

STORY #6. Paparazzi- Get the Picture

My friend, DR, shared a story of a friend-ship that was intense but short lived. She called it; "You can't handle the truth." She and KM were friends for less than a year. They were both living in LA at the time, had fast-paced careers, were young and had the world as their 'oyster'.

They were training together for a marathon so were very dedicated to helping each other out. Being young, they partied a lot, shopped a lot and went for coffee - a lot. KM shared stories of her troubled relationship with DR. Her boy-friend was a photographer for a National maga-zine and was, by profession, a 'Paparazzi'. KM would complain that he mistreated her and he wouldn't pay for anything they did together. DR wasn't (still isn't) one to mince her words. So she finally said to her then friend - "You don't want to be in a relationship that is toxic. You're playing second fiddle to him, why would you do that?"

Shortly after that chat, KM dropped their relationship, like a hot potato. Turns out, KM wanted a friend to listen without response. Without action. Without judgement.

Did DR do anything wrong? Not really. Did KM over-react? Hard to say. We shouldn't stand in judgement of either of their actions. "When the student is ready, the teacher appears." Sometimes, when we think we are helping, our friends think we are over-stepping.

They aren't ready to hear the 'truth'. Hopefully, KM was able to resolve her problems, but we may never know.

Break it down even more.

Have you ever had a friend like DR or KM? Are you one of them now? If so, which one? Jot down their name(s). _____

_____

_____

_____

How could you approach your friend if you believe their love relationship is in jeopardy?

_____

_____

_____

_____

If your friend were to approach you with opinions about your love relationship, how would you react? _____

_____

_____

_____

Have you ever felt this way about any of your friendships? Have you thought that it was more one-sided because you did most of the 'heavy-lifting', so to speak, to keep it going?

List the things that you do that outweigh what your friend does. What heavy-lifting are you doing that your friend is not?

_____

_____

_____

_____

_____

_____

_____

_____

08

The Anatomy of a Friendship –

Fluidity Explored

"Your circle should want to see you win. Your circle should clap loudly when you have good news. If not, get a new circle."

- Anon

The Anatomy of a Friendship - Fluidity Explored

By now, we should begin to understand that friendship is more fluid than it is static. By this I mean that friendships change. People change. Everything changes! Are you the same person you were when you were 20? 30? 50+? The answer is simple, no. How could you be with all that goes into making a person? Arguably, we could say that many of our core values might be the same, but who we are and what we want out of life changes-constantly. With that in mind, how can we expect anyone to stay the same throughout their lifetime? Let's take a closer look at the anatomy of friendships and their subsequent fluidity.

A common example is marriage/partner-ships. Many people marry the 'loves of their lives'. Right? I think you know where I am going with this. We all start out with idealized thoughts about our chosen partners. We adore everything about them like their cute sneeze, the way he puts on his t-shirt, how the toilet seat remains up after use (it's a guy thing), or how she takes an hour to put on her makeup. I've heard so often that, 'he's my best friend' or she's my 'soul mate', and yet how long before you start to hear or say, "You've changed, why can't you be like when we first met?" Really? R-e-a-l-l-y?

In North America, the average length of time a marriage lasts is 7 years and 50% end in divorce! WTF? This doesn't even take into account the people who live in common-law relationships and separate. These partnerships are not recorded. Wow! Hard to absorb.

Another common example is your BFF (best friend forever).

Put their name here _____

How long have you been friends?_____

What type of person is she/he? (Describe in point form) _____

_____

_____

_____

Imagine for a moment when you first met. How did you feel around them? How do you feel around them now? What has changed?

I'm going to assume that a number of things have been fluid. As we move through our lives and mature we are met with thousands of external changes to our environment, our families and our physical being. Perhaps, we have moved, changed jobs, had kids, changed political views and maybe even faith. I think you get the picture. Your BFF has also been through these changes. So it stands to reason that as you both face change and adapt to life on a daily basis, your relationship has shifted and adapted as well. I will say for the better, otherwise, you really can't call them a best friend, now can you?

Some accepted ideals of friendship can include, pleasure felt when you are in contact, reciprocity, commitment, and mutual respect. We often feel love for these people. A give-and-take relationship is formed and support for one another is expected to flow both ways.

I've often been asked, how many friends should one have? There is no real answer to this question, however, research has done some work for us. It is estimated that having between three to five close friends is optimal for one's own happiness. While this might be a surprise to some, the key word here is -'close'. It is widely accepted that people have more friends that they associate with, but the value of these peripheral friends gets diluted the farther away they are from your inner 'tribe'. Imagine a circle of people holding hands as in the picture below.

Your closest friends are in the inner circle or what we are referring to as our 'tribe'. These people know our deep, dark secrets. They know our history. They sit with us at our dinner table or drink wine late into the night.

The next row represents those people that you might extend an invite to a BBQ party or your 'coffee' only friends. The last row would be those people we call 'associated' or 'peripheral' friends and are often 'friends of friends'.

The fluidity of the outer two circles is higher than the inner one. These circles tend to change often as they are not associated with core values or love for one another. Some people believe all these circles are their 'tribe'. Wrong! Why, you ask? Because the amount of investment you have with the inner tribe far outweighs that of the outer circles. It is both physically and emotionally impossible to keep that many people close to you. And I can assure you that those people feel the same way. Guaranteed.

Allow me to demonstrate. My most recent example of this is when I met a woman a few years ago and we became fast friends. We had a lot in common, still do. We even worked together on various projects and had a lot of laughs. Still do. But what changed? We both had parents that were diagnosed with cancer and within a short time, they both passed away. Although we were both supportive of each other, we sought comfort from others. These 'others' were our tribe members. We knew we had to cut each other some slack and allow the time necessary to deal with caring for our parents. This wasn't the time to 'fertilize' our friendship. It was time to have mutual respect and understanding for each other.

After our parents passing, we never got back to the close friendship we had prior to these events. Why? I found it difficult to be her close friend because I didn't know how to. Something changed. But I grew to accept it because I knew in my heart, that she and I would be ok. Our friendship is important, but liquid. I'm ok with that. I think she is too.

09

Gardening Tips –
Soil, Nutrients, Fertilizer, Etc.

"Tears you share with friends only help water your garden."

- Diana Ruff

Gardening Tips: Soil, Nutrients, Fertilizer, Etc.

As this book comes to a close, I wanted say a few words about my 'garden'.

Over the many years I've been here on Earth, my 'garden' has changed countless times. It has been met with drought, an over abundance of unwanted weeds, and has lacked fertilizer and nutrients at times. But did that ever stop my green thumb from working? Did I shrivel up and die? Was I added to the compost pile? NO! NO! And NO!

Quite the contrary. I have been blessed with some amazing 'flowers' in my life. I have learned that sometimes we need to choose the right seeds to plant in our soil.

At birth, our 'soil' starts off with plenty of rich nutrients, sunlight and water. Overtime, if we don't tend to our gardens regularly, we can face an overgrown mess of weeds, roots, and depleted soil. While some of us might give up before we even get the hoe out, most of us are not willing to settle.

Your garden needs nutrients. It needs fertilizer to grow strong, healthy plants and flowers. As your garden needs regular tending, so do your friends. Friends deserve your time, your love, your 'friendship'. Without your attention, your friends, will whither away. Take the onus upon yourself and remember these simple but impactful words from one clever woman, Hanna Galsby,

"It's not the garden, but the gardening that counts."

Stay Calm and Weed on! slb

Manufactured by Amazon.ca
Bolton, ON

35385701R00063